ODD LAWS

Legal Lunacy
from around the World

JENNY PASCHALL and RON LYON

Illustrated by Andy Hunt

HarperCollins*Publishers*

HarperCollins*Publishers*
77–85 Fulham Palace Road,
Hammersmith, London W6 8JB

A Paperback Original 1996
1 3 5 7 9 8 6 4 2

Copyright © Jenny Paschall 1996
Illustrations © Andy Hunt 1996

Jenny Paschall asserts the moral right to
be identified as the author of this work

A catalogue record for this book
is available from the British Library

ISBN 0 00 638713 6

Photoset in Linotron Goudy Old Style by
Rowland Phototypesetting Limited
Bury St Edmunds, Suffolk

Printed and bound in Great Britain by
Caledonian International Book Manufacturing Ltd
Glasgow

CONTENTS

ODD·LAWS

CHAPTER 1

One For The Road

'One for the road' always seemed to be such a friendly farewell, at least before the drink driving laws were enforced. In fact, the phrase has a much more sinister meaning, originating from the days of public hangings. When a condemned prisoner left Newgate Prison on his way to the gibbet, he would be put on a cart which would stop at every pub along the route. Each publican would give the prisoner a free drink – *One for the Road*. Usually by the time the gibbet and the hangman came into view, the condemned man was far too drunk to care about his fate.

Love-struck drivers beware: the lawmakers have considered you when devising codes for the roads. Drivers in Leighton Buzzard, Bedfordshire, for example, are prohibited from kissing a companion while driving on winding roads – obviously you're safe to snog as long as the road ahead is straight! In Detroit, Michigan, it is illegal to make love in a car unless it is parked on the couple's own property, while taxi drivers who have sex in the front seat of their vehicles during their working shifts are breaking the law in Springfield, Massachusetts.

In Bologna, Italy, a special law applies to prostitutes who drive. It states that a prostitute can, 'drive a car carefully and at the same time lead a scandalous life'.

Bologna isn't the only city to concern itself with the decency of its drivers. In Athens it is illegal to operate a motor vehicle on public roads if you are 'poorly dressed' or 'un-bathed'. The law-makers of Pocatello, Idaho, have taken things one step further, issuing a law that reads: 'It is prohibited for pedestrians and motorists to display frowns, grimaces, scowls, threatening and glowering looks, gloomy and depressed facial appearances, generally all of which reflect unfavourably upon the city's reputation.'

In Springfield, Ohio, it is unlawful to clean and dust the interior of a car while it is being driven down a city street.

You can always trust an Irishman to come up with a good excuse. One gentleman from Galway failed to show up in court after being caught travelling at seventy-seven m.p.h. down a quiet country road. When tracked down, he claimed that the summons got lost in the wash. While the judge sympathetically agreed that it could happen to anyone, it didn't stop her finding him guilty.

Englishman Barry Saville went one better when he was taken to court for driving over the limit. He claimed it was the paraffin he used in his stage act as a fire-eater that caused the positive reaction in the breathalyser, not alcohol at all. Magistrates adjourned the case to allow him to recreate his act at a London Hospital and prove his innocence.

Double parking in Minneapolis, Minnesota, could be just the ticket if you are trying to lose weight. The legal punishment is time on a chain gang, being fed only bread and water. Or you could take a walk across the street in Swat, in the Himalayas, where jaywalkers are forced to run along the road until they fall over from exhaustion. But if you're really desperate, try visiting Hammond, Indiana, where the automatic penalty for littering the street is one good dose of castor oil to be administered by the police department. A punishment sure to get criminals on the run!

Most countries take driving while drunk seriously, but the punishments can vary enormously. In Turkey, a drunk driver can be driven twenty miles outside the town, then forced to walk back to town under the supervision of police officers.

In Switzerland, if you wear glasses, it is mandatory to keep an extra pair in the car at all times. If, however, they are reading glasses, they will be useless in Norman, Oklahoma, where it is illegal to read a comic while driving a car.

When Patricia Wakelin advertised her Ford Fiesta for sale, she ended up with more than she bargained for. A man arrived to see the car, apologising for bringing his grandmother with him. He took the car for a test drive, leaving his Skoda and his granny behind as collateral – and never came back. When the police investigated, they found that the Skoda was stolen, and the lady was from a nearby old people's home. She thought she was being taken out for a drive by a friendly young gentleman called Dave whom she had never seen before.

9

Drivers in Pennsylvania had better be well equipped. The law states: 'Any motorist driving along a country road at night must stop every mile and send up a rocket signal, wait ten minutes for the road to be cleared of livestock, and then continue . . . Any motorist who sights a team of horses coming towards him must pull well off the road, cover his car with a blanket or canvas that blends with the countryside, and let the horses pass. If the horses appear skittish, the motorist must take his car apart, piece by piece, and hide it under the nearest bushes.'

If you're driving through Pleasantville, Iowa, at night, be sure your car is preceded by a man carrying a red lantern or you will be breaking the law.

A New York State Vehicle and Traffic Law makes the following bewildering pronouncement: 'Two vehicles which are passing each other in opposite directions shall have the right of way.'

An Oklahoma law reads: 'The driver of any vehicle involved in an accident resulting in death shall immediately stop and give his name and address to the person struck.'

'Whoever operates an automobile or motorcycle on any public way – laid out under authority of law recklessly or while under the influence of liquor shall be punished,' states a law in Massachusetts, thereby imposing upon the poor motorist the duty of finding out whether the workers who built the road he intends to use were drunk or careless.

Perhaps the American lawmakers should take a leaf out of the book of the Lebanese and make their road laws a bit more reader-friendly . . . No harsh words of warning there, the road signs are wonderfully polite. Take this speed restriction, for example: 'Proceed Most Awfully Slowly – Fifteen Miles to the Hour'. In Tokyo they even provide a translation of the rules of the road for English-speaking drivers. 'When a passenger of the foot moves into sight,' states one such translation, 'tootie the horn trumpet. If he still obstacles your passage, tootie him with vigour and express by word of mouth warning, "Hi!".'

When a lorry overturned in Hampshire, the local police found a novel way of cooling the heated tempers of the drivers stuck in the ensuing traffic jam. They handed out tubs of ice cream – the overturned lorry was carrying seven tons of the stuff.

Taxi drivers may think they are above the law but they had better not keep their passengers above them in Youngstown, Ohio, where it is illegal for a taxi to carry passengers on the roof.

A taxi driver in Prague who turns the meter rate to level three (three times faster than the legal rate of one) is breaking the law UNLESS the ride is taking place following a nuclear explosion. Then the *sazba*, or rate, of three is officially sanctioned by the Government.

Road hogs aren't the only animals to avoid on the highway. In Utah, a local edict allows birds the right of way on all streets. Dogs cannot ride in ambulances in Westport, Massachusetts, however, while in Missouri it is illegal for uncaged bears to ride in a car or be carried in the boot.

'It is mandatory for a motorist with criminal intentions to stop at the city limits and telephone the chief of police as he is entering the town,' cautions an ordinance in Tacoma, Washington.

A traffic warden in Southsea, Hampshire, has been awarded a police commendation certificate, normally reserved for officers who have performed acts of bravery. So what did Angela Hallam do to deserve such an award? Had she tackled armed robbers, or saved the life of a drowning man? No, nothing so mundane. She was honoured for issuing 4,071 fixed penalty fines in one year. Local drivers celebrated by parking on yellow lines while the wonder warden was attending the presentation ceremony.

Perhaps they should send her on a long vacation. How about Milwaukee, where a car parked for more than two hours must be securely tied to a horse?

Elephants tied to parking meters in Orlando, Florida, must feed the meter the same parking fee as that required for an automobile. Mrs Silvia Matos could have bought several elephants with the amount of parking meter fines she paid in New York City. Between 1985 and 1988 she received 2,800 parking tickets, resulting in penalties totalling $150,000.

Here's a statistic for British women drivers to memorise: ninety-two per cent of drivers driving recklessly, causing death or bodily harm, driving while under the influence of alcohol or drugs, breaking speed limits, causing accidents, neglecting signs, directions or pedestrian rights, or driving carelessly, are . . . male.

13

Everybody hates a back-seat driver, but in London they can actually be prosecuted, since there is a law stating that drivers must be sitting in the front seat whilst driving.

Adam Greenwood of Burnley, Lancashire, went on a night's drinking binge and stole a twenty-five-tonne mechanical excavator because he missed the last bus home. Unable to drive the huge vehicle with any semblance of control, he caused over £50,000 worth of damage, destroying a twenty-tonne weigh-bridge, two offices and several trees.

No clever cycling stunts in Denver, Colorado, please! It is illegal to lift your feet higher than the front of the bicycle when riding down this city's streets.

The first ever speed traps were set up in England in 1902. Police would hide behind hedges with a bicycle and stop-watch, ready to jump out and pursue errant drivers. One of the earliest offenders was Lord Montagu of Beaulieu, who was caught going more than twelve m.p.h.

California's El Dorado County had a rather peculiar attitude towards speeding. Legislation written in 1907 stated: 'Speed upon county roads will be limited to ten miles an hour unless the motorist sees a bailiff who does not appear to have had a drink in thirty days, then the driver will be permitted to make what he can.'

Diving and/or fishing from a motor-boat while driving down a city street is illegal in Brewton, Alabama.

A hearse driver was arrested for speeding and dangerous driving in Foligno, Italy. The funeral procession was forced to follow as he sped to the church with the coffin bouncing up and down behind. The undertaker said he wanted to unload the body and get to a football match.

In Memphis, Tennessee, it is forbidden to drive a car while the driver is asleep, while in South Dakota and Oklahoma it illegal to sleep in the middle of the road.

Firemen going to or from a fire on a bicycle in Hiawatha, Kansas, have right of way on the pavement.

Perhaps the most sensible driving ordinance is that enforced in Birmingham, Alabama, where it is illegal to drive a car while blindfolded.

The Malaysians obviously believe that women drive their men to drink, since the innocent wife of a drunk driver faces a jail sentence there.

Suspicious police in Jackson, Mississippi, stopped a car that was being driven erratically and discovered the driver was blind. There was, however, a simple explanation – he was being directed by his friend sitting in the passenger seat who admitted he was too drunk to drive himself.

CHAPTER 2

The Eye Of The Beholder

In some places, just being overweight or ugly is likely to cause a brush with the law. In Tropea, Italy, for instance, women are not allowed to appear nude on a beach if they are 'fat, ugly, or generally unattractive'. The law specifies that nude sunbathing is permitted only by 'young women capable of exalting the beauty of the female body'.

The lawmakers of Kentucky have decreed that: 'No female shall appear in a bathing suit on any highway within the Commonwealth of Kentucky unless she be escorted by at least two officers or unless she be armed with a club.' A subsequent amendment states: '. . . the provisions of this statute shall not apply to females weighing less than ninety pounds nor exceeding 200 pounds nor shall it apply to female horses.'

Richard Plant, twenty-nine, was charged with indecency by police in Johannesburg. He was arrested by traffic police who found him undressed from the waist down, but he was acquitted after he explained that his girlfriend was sitting on his lap at the time, and was therefore hiding his nudity.

Women in Gurnee, Illinois weighing fourteen stone or more cannot wear shorts when riding a horse.

In Palermo, Italy, it is the men who have to be careful – women can sunbathe nude in public whenever they want, but men are subject to a fine. The law states: 'The male anatomical conformation can become obscene, even unconsciously.'

Until 1936 it was illegal for men to wear topless bathing suits in New York. In 1934, eight men were fined $1 each for topless bathing at Coney Island! In 1935 there was a mass arrest of forty-two topless male bathers in Atlantic City.

CHAPTER 3

Love And Marriage . . .

A Greek man cannot promise to marry a girl in order to seduce her. If this happens, the man must compensate the girl for the loss of her virginity.

The well-dressed Roman bride would not want to be seen with anything on her head – except cake! The custom of breaking the wedding cake over the bride's head was an essential part of the ceremony as, by law, only children born of a bride who took part in this would be eligible in later life to assume high office.

In Seattle, Washington, a female may ride on a bus or train while sitting on a man's lap if she first places a pillow between herself and the offending lap.

In Kentucky, it is illegal for a man to marry his wife's grandmother. Any chance of this law being broken in South Dakota is greatly reduced, because there women over fifty cannot go for a walk and initiate a conversation with a married man over twenty.

In Indiana and Ohio it is a felony for a skating teacher to attempt to seduce a female student.

On 21 November, 1988, François Arsonval walked into a Paris police station and gave himself up. He was wanted for theft and bigamy, and finally confessed to marrying no less than 185 women in twelve years. The cases have still not been heard; police are having difficulty tracing all the women. This case would probably have amused Lord Russell of Killowen, a respected Lord Chief Justice of England. When he was asked what was the maximum punishment for bigamy his reply was, 'Two mothers-in-law'!

Montana legislators have made it a felony for a wife to open her husband's mail.

Law-makers in Peace Dale, Rhode Island, have declared it illegal for any female to be given a cigarette by a man. In Corvallis, Oregon, young ladies cannot drink any coffee after six p.m. If a woman is trying to give up cigarettes and coffee, she would do well to avoid visiting Pocatello, Idaho, where it is illegal to look gloomy in public!

But, here's a law of which feminists would approve. In Cold Spring, Pennsylvania, liquor can only be sold to a married man if his wife has given her written permission. Kentucky women can have even more fun. They are actually encouraged by law to spike their husband's alcoholic drinks with castor oil to curtail their drinking. Welcome to the Whiskey-a-go-go!

Ohio statutes permit a woman to burn her husband's old clothing.

In Whitesville, Delaware, they are trying to nip domestic unrest in the bud. In fact, a woman can be arrested for disturbing the peace . . . by merely proposing marriage to a man! In Dyersburg, Tennessee, it is illegal for a girl even to phone a man for a date.

A matchmaker in Guangzhou Province, China, is on trial for fraud. It seems he convinced a barber to offer his unwilling wife for a scam in which they would sell the woman to a farmer, collect the fee, then immediately retrieve her. The arrangement backfired on nearly all counts. The barber was cheated out of the promised reward and now faces life in prison for selling his wife. The matchmaker also faces life imprisonment. Ironically, the fraudulent matchmaker had been an excellent judge of character. The wife preferred the farmer and refused to return to the barber.

In Baluchistan, Pakistan, a man can legally exchange his sister for a wife. For years a Pennsylvania husband could beat his wife, but not until after ten p.m., and in Alabama it was legal until 1871 for a man to choke his wife – with no time restrictions!

A woman in India can legally marry a goat. Some women may be forgiven for thinking that this is not restricted to India.

In Wichita, Kansas, a husband is allowed to mistreat his mother-in-law.

Men in Portland, Maine, cannot tickle a woman under the chin with a feather duster – no mention is made of other parts of the anatomy.

In Finland no one is allowed to marry until they can read.

. . . AND SEX

Alaskan police, acting on a tip, raided the hotel room of an Oregon man in which they found cocaine and $10,000 in cash. When asked why he had such a large amount of cash, he said it was given to him by a woman, whose name he had forgotten, as a reward for great sex.

A condom manufacturer decided to call his new range 'Stealth Condoms'. The Northrop Corporation, builder of the B–2 'Stealth Bomber', filed suit, claiming that people might confuse the two products. They were presumably protecting customers seeking the ultimate big bang!

Dr Alan Maryon Davies was accused of sexual harassment after telling a lady colleague, 'I'm a bottom man myself'. He explained that there were no sexual undertones to his comment, however: they were on a train and had just passed through a town called Pratt's Bottom, which had prompted him to make this confession.

Poor Gloria Sykes was hit by a cable car, and sued the San Francisco cable car company. Her claim was a little unusual, however. She was not particularly concerned by the cuts and bruises she suffered – she filed suit claiming that the accident had left her with serious psychological and neurological damage, which caused her to become a nymphomaniac. As a result, she said, she had engaged in sexual relations with over one hundred men. The court awarded her $50,000 damages.

Let's hope she doesn't make a trip to Rhode Island, where it was proposed that there should be a two-dollar tax levied on every act of sexual intercourse.

In England it is against the law to kiss in a cinema or to embrace in the street, while in London you cannot make love in trains, buses, parked cars, churchyards, churches or parks.

In Riverside, California, kissing is illegal – unless both parties first wipe their lips with rose water. In Halethorpe, Maryland, you don't need rose water but a stopwatch to remain on the right side of the law – it is illegal to kiss for more than one second. And just in case you wonder how seriously these laws were treated, in the eighteenth century a sea captain in Boston was sentenced to spend two hours in the stocks for kissing his wife in public on a Sunday after returning from three years at sea.

Still more kissing – in Indiana, anyone who sports a moustache and who 'habitually kisses human beings' is breaking the law.

CHAPTER 4

Till Death Us Do Part

Ian Bell, a carpet-fitter from Rotherham, South Yorkshire, claimed in the divorce courts that his wife's possessiveness was making his life unbearable. He told the court how his wife had made him move house because attractive women lived on the street and forced him into their bedroom whenever neighbours were sunbathing. He also related how he finally lost his temper and threw a plant at her. Bell pleaded guilty to causing his wife actual bodily harm with a rubber plant, but was released after the court was shown photographs of the injuries he sustained from the fight.

The newest problem being dealt with in American divorce courts is custody of the pets. US lawyers are reaping massive fees for dragging domestic animals through America's court-rooms to decide which party is best for the animal's interests. The United States Humane Society has warned that the pets may suffer from post-divorce depression. One couple, however, managed to compromise – they decided amicably that neither party was more deserving of custody – so they had their dachshund put down.

Lars Jonsson refused to join his wife in attending a demonstration against domestic violence in Stockholm. His wife, Anne, felt it was only right that she should have her man at her side to show domestic unity – so she tried to convince him to accompany her. Unfortunately, her methods were a little extreme and Lars ended up in hospital with a fractured skull as a result of the beating she gave him.

In Sicily, it was once customary to bite off your spouse's nose if she was unfaithful.

Sometimes the smallest incident can lead to murder. A Parisian night-watchman, Noel Carriou, broke his wife's neck because she under-cooked his roast dinner. He served a twelve-year sentence for the crime (possibly the judge shared his passion for good food and felt Monsieur Carriou had some cause for anger). He was released after seven years, and subsequently remarried. Unfortunately wife number two burnt the roast, so Carriou stabbed her. He received an eight-year sentence. Perhaps he should have tried wooing Delia Smith!

Stuart Dingley of Dudley, West Midlands, stabbed his girlfriend to death when she switched off the television during an FA Cup Final replay.

When Mrs Anne Bass, the former wife of a Texas millionaire, was offered a divorce settlement of $535 million, she turned it down. She claimed it was not enough to keep her in the style to which she had become accustomed.

Divorced couples in Vancouver now have the opportunity to remove their exes from their lives forever. Divorce X will remove the image of your former spouse from family photographs and replace it with pleasant scenery. The service costs about $100 per photograph. It is also possible to fill the space with a new lover.

In Saudi Arabia, if a man does not provide his wife with regular amounts of coffee, she can divorce him.

Nina Housden was certainly a cool-headed murderess. She fell asleep in the front seat of her car while it was being repaired in a garage in Toledo – seemingly unconcerned that her husband's dismembered corpse, wrapped in Christmas paper, was on the back seat. The grisly package was discovered by the mechanic, who called the police. Nina was awoken and arrested.

CHAPTER 5

House Rules

In Rumford, Maine, it is against the law to bite your landlord.

It is illegal for a married couple to live in an abandoned bus in Upton on Severn.

Housewives in Pittsburgh, Pennsylvania, are banned from hiding dirt and dust under a rug.

Californian housewives must boil their dusters after use. Failure to do so could result in a fine or jail.

In 1937 spring cleaning became compulsory in Hungary. All lofts, garrets and cellars had to be spring cleaned. Fines were imposed on citizens who did not comply.

A law in Baltimore, Maryland, makes it illegal to clean a sink, no matter how dirty or stained it may be.

In Portland, Oregon, you are breaking the law if you shake a feather duster in another person's face.

Legislators in Nappanee, Indiana, have decreed that washing lines must be less than fifty inches in length, and women must never hang their underwear outside at any time. Scranton, Pennsylvania, doesn't care how long the line is but if women are hanging their underwear outside to dry, there has to be a fence high enough to screen the undies from neighbours and passers-by. In Los Angeles women can hang their laundry outside openly in the summer, but not at all in winter.

Taking a bath prior to ten p.m. is strictly illegal in Piqua, Ohio; codes in Clinton, Indiana, declare that it is illegal to bathe at any hour during the winter; and in the State of Virginia and Topeka, Kansas, it's against the law to put a bathtub in a house.

In New York City it is illegal to carry a skeleton into a tenement building.

Clean Air Act? Every citizen of Kentucky is required by law to take a bath once a year. The residents of Barre, Vermont, are far more clean living, since they must bathe at least once a week to stay on the right side of the law.

In Kidderminster it is an offence to own a bath without a watertight plug. In Dallas, Texas it is illegal to have a leaking tap.

In Portland, Oregon, its unlawful to bathe without wearing suitable clothing – bathers must be covered from neck to knees.

In Stanford, North Carolina, a man drove to City Hall wearing only a towel, to complain that his water had just been shut off in the middle of his shower. After the city pointed out that his account was overdue and that it had mailed two warnings, the dripping-wet complainant stood in line, paid his bill, and returned home to finish his shower.

Until the nineteenth century, baths in Spain were illegal because they were said to be a heathen abomination.

In Pueblo, Colorado, it is against the law to raise or permit a dandelion to grow within the city limits.

New York City and Santa Fe, New Mexico, forbid lawn mowing on the Sabbath. Finding a lawn in New York City would be a trick on any day, let alone mowing one.

Don't call the police if you hear heavy blows in the night in San Francisco – it's probably only a carpet that's taking a beating. It is illegal to beat a rug on a city pavement of that city at any time *except* between midnight and eight a.m. However, while the denizens of San Francisco can stand out on the street beating their carpets to a pulp all night, they had better not get out the sweeper – sweeping a carpet between twelve and eight can land you in jail!

31

Port Jervis, New York, has declared it against the law to spread a rug or carpet on a city street. The citizens of Cleveland, Ohio, cannot beat or shake a rug close to any building occupied by more than one family.

It is illegal to stack more than eight dishes in any one pile anywhere in Kansas, while Freeport, Illinois, prohibits tossing dishes out of the windows of any upper-storey apartment or second storey of a house.

The Ten Commandments state we should not covet our neighbour's wife; Florida law goes one further, and decrees it is illegal to offer a job to your neighbour's cook.

New Orleans has made kicking garbage cans a crime. In Seattle, Washington, it is illegal to remove the lids of garbage cans without the permission of the owners or the city fathers. In Montgomery, Alabama, it's illegal to sit on a garbage can, while citizens of Savannah, Georgia, must not toss rubbish bins out of a second-floor window.

Pittsburgh, Pennsylvania, prohibits snoozing in a refrigerator, while in Detroit, Michigan it is illegal to snooze in a bath, and in Lubbock, Texas, you can be fined if found sleeping in a garbage can.

In San Jose, California, you would be breaking the law if you slept in a neighbour's outside toilet without his permission. A night in jail would be a pleasant alternative.

Savannah Beach, Georgia, and Cambridge, Massachusetts, have made it unlawful to snore in a bedroom unless the windows are closed and securely locked.

Professor Trevor Kirkham of Montreal University decided to sue the former owner of the house he bought in Lancashire, because it was not haunted. He says he was misled into buying the £420,000 house by the former owner, who claimed it was haunted by the spirit of the English martyr John Wall. Professor Kirkham discovered later that John Wall never set foot in the area and was buried by nuns in East Anglia. Perhaps he should have asked his surveyor to check the house with a spirit level.

Huntingdon, West Virginia, officially frowns upon one family sharing a rubbish bin with another.

In Canton, Ohio ownership of baths is illegal.

Poor Mary Carruthers of Dorset was evicted because she was Jim Reeves's number one fan. Neighbours complained that all they could hear all day long was Jim Reeves records played on full volume. The problem was so bad that the council finally evicted her on the grounds of mental cruelty to her neighbours.

The last word in security blankets? Americans have become so concerned about being shot in their beds by armed burglars that a US security company has come up with the answer – special bullet-proof duvets are now on sale in all good appliance stores and gun shops.

CHAPTER 6

A Close Shave

Barbers in Omaha, Nebraska, are forbidden by law from shaving a customer's chest, while in Carrizozo, New Mexico, women are *required* by law to shave their legs as well as their face.

Ordinances in Morrisville, Pennsylvania, prohibit men from being shaved by someone else as well as requiring a permit in order for them to shave themselves. Practising some sort of gender equality, Morrisville also requires its womenfolk to buy a special permit if they wish to wear cosmetics.

In Waterloo, Nebraska, barbers cannot eat onions between seven a.m. and seven p.m. Disregarding this law can result in a fine and closing of the shop.

Barbers using a brush on a customer's hair are breaking the law in Tennessee, while in Hawaii barbers cannot use a shaving brush to lather a customer's chin. Non-compliance could result in a brush with the law!

Massachusetts citizens cannot shave while driving a car. That state also prohibits men having their hair dyed or permed in a beauty salon.

In 1838 the King of Bavaria decreed that civilians were forbidden from wearing moustaches, and commanded the police to arrest and cause to be shaved the offending parties.

The school board of Binghamton, New York, has made it illegal to enter a school room with a moustache.

In Tanzania men cannot have hair more than two inches long, while women cannot wear wigs or excessive make-up. The penalty for first-time offenders is a warning, a haircut and four strokes of the cane. Repeat offenders can be given jail sentences ranging from six months to life.

Arkansas teachers cannot have their hair bobbed. Those who do will forfeit their pay rise.

Hair transplants can be more dangerous than you may imagine – in New York, bald men who visit hairdressers to have their hair re-grown are breaking the law.

If your child needs a haircut, perhaps you should avoid finding a barber from Elkhart, Indiana, where it was necessary to pass a law prohibiting barbers from threatening to cut off a child's ears.

When Mark Barnsley had his hair cut, the results were not quite what he expected. In fact, he thought he looked like a convict. Which was particularly unfortunate because he had been given the haircut whilst on remand in Doncaster Jail. Mr Barnsley took the issue to court, claiming that his appearance would jeopardise his chance of a fair trial. The judge agreed that he had been given a shaven head against his wishes, awarded him £100 damages, and ruled that the prison would pay all costs. Barnsley was nicknamed 'Baldman of Doncatraz' by his fellow inmates.

When Victoria Baldwin had a haircut in Sydney, Australia, she was so upset with her new look that she sued. She claimed that the hairdresser had cut her hair too short, which made her look like Hillary Clinton. The sympathetic court agreed, and awarded her £320 for psychological damage and another £100 for her to buy hats to cover her hair until it grew. The psychological damage of the case on the real Mrs Clinton has yet to be assessed.

CHAPTER 7

When In Rome, or Holiday Hazards

Holiday-makers in Kenya should refrain from joining in the fun if the locals decide to strip off their clothes and streak. It is perfectly permissible for Kenyans, but foreign streakers are breaking the law.

Salem, Massachusetts, known in the past for being inhospitable to witches, has an edict declaring it illegal for travellers and holiday-makers to sleep nude in a rented room – even if they are married.

It is illegal to mispronounce the name of the city of Joliet, Illinois.

Visitors to New York City should beware of making rude gestures – they could be breaking the law. It's still on the statute books that, 'It is disorderly conduct for one man to greet another on the street by placing the end of his thumb against the tip of his nose, at the same time extending and wriggling the fingers of his hand.'

In Palma, Majorca, a group of helpers accompanying a party of disabled travellers were made to dance and run around before Spanish airline officials would allow them to board a flight. Spanish law dictates that no more than seven per cent of passengers may be disabled. The aides were made to sprint around the aircraft aisles and perform dances before being allowed passage.

In Pennsylvania it is against the law to speak loudly at picnics.

CHAPTER 8

Eat, Drink – And Be Arrested

Doughnut lovers should avoid Oak Park, Illinois, where the law restricts the making of doughnuts to *no more than one hundred per person per day*.

Brenda L Hunter, of Zion, Illinois, shot her brother because she did not like the kind of cheese he was putting on their chilli dinner.

The Chinese invented a novel method of lie detection – chewing rice. The accused was given a handful of dry rice to eat. The theory was that a guilty person would have a dry mouth and would be unable to swallow, whereas an innocent person would not be nervous and so would have more saliva in his mouth.

Carmel, California, had a law forbidding ice cream parlours, until Clint Eastwood became the mayor. The outlaw ice cream lover proclaimed that the town wasn't big enough for both of them, so the law went!

In sixteenth- and seventeenth-century Turkey, caffeine really was bad for your health since anyone caught drinking coffee was put to death.

It was once against the law in Cambodia to insult a rice plant. Could that have anything to do with the first cereal killer?

In Lexington, Kentucky, it is illegal to carry an ice cream cone in your pocket. Is that an ice cream cone in your pocket, or are you just glad to see me?

A Scottish law reads as follows: 'In the Nuts (unground), (other than ground nuts) Order, the expression nuts shall have reference to such nuts, other than ground nuts, as would but for this amending order not qualify as nuts (unground) (other than ground nuts) by reason of their being nuts (unground).' How's that for a nutty law?

Dorothy Parker claimed that 'Candy is dandy', but beware, it can cause legal problems. In Idaho, a citizen is forbidden by law to give another citizen a box of candy that weighs more than fifty pounds.

For diabetic con man Leo Koretz, candy was not so much dandy as lethal. When he was jailed after a long career of embezzlement and fraud, he decided that prison was not for him and that he would commit suicide. He induced a girl-friend to bring him a five-pound box of chocolates, which he ate entirely on 9 January, 1925 – and promptly died.

When sixteen-year-old Stephen Dennison stole a box of chocolates from a New York shop in 1925, he had little idea what the future would hold. He was sent to the state reformatory, where he remained for two years. He was then transferred to the state penitentiary, where he broke a number of minor rules over a period of time – each misdemeanour adding time to his sentence. He was eventually released in 1959, after spending thirty-four years in prison for stealing five dollars' worth of sweets.

In Cleveland, Ohio, it is illegal for more than one person to sip from the same bottle of whisky, while a LeFors, Texas, ordinance makes it illegal to take more than three swallows of beer at any one time while standing. In Chicago, it is illegal to drink at all standing up, but in St Louis, Missouri, codes forbid the drinking of beer sitting down on the kerb of a city street.

Waitresses in Topeka, Kansas, cannot serve wine in a teacup. Nebraska restaurants cannot serve beer or wine unless there is a large pot of hot soup cooking. In New Jersey restaurants it is illegal to slurp soup, whether or not you drink wine or beer.

In Saskatchewan, Canada, it is illegal to drink water in beer parlours, which is a law Tommy Johns of Brisbane, Australia, would never have broken. By the time he died at the age of sixty-six, he had been arrested almost 3,000 times for drunkenness.

It is illegal to gargle publicly in either Louisiana or Hot Springs, Arkansas.

In Marblehead, Massachusetts, each fire company is entitled to a three-gallon jug of rum after responding to a fire alarm. If your house catches fire, you'd better hope it's the first call of the night!

In Indiana it is against the law to travel on a bus within four hours of eating garlic. Rumour has it the bill was initiated by a pale and quite obscure state legislator from Transylvania.

Restaurateurs in New York were for many years the victims of a Mafia parsley racket. They were forced to buy 'mob' parsley to use as garnish for the meals they served. The price rose from five cents to forty cents a bunch, and some restaurateurs found their parsley bill amounting to $150 a month. In the early 1980s, a number of the victimised restaurant owners hit on a money-saving tactic – since no one ever ate the parsley, they instructed waiters to take it off the finished plates, wash it and re-use it. A seventy-five-year-old Mafia boss nicknamed Un Occhio (One Eye) caught on to this. Rather than openly threaten the owners, he claimed to be disgusted by this unhygienic practice and expressed outrage to the restaurants in question, who promptly ordered vast quantities of fresh parsley. Coincidentally, One Eye is reputed to control vast acres of parsley in California, producing enough parsley for the needs of the entire United States.

Ministers in Marion, Oregon, who eat garlic or wild onions before preaching a sermon could be in trouble not only with their parishioners but with local authorities, as well.

Hawaiian women used to face the death penalty for eating coconuts.

Mourners attending a wake in Boston cannot eat more than three sandwiches.

In Detroit, Michigan, you can be arrested if caught throwing banana skins on a public thoroughfare, while in California it is illegal to peel an orange in a hotel room. Worse still, anyone caught stealing citrus fruit in Yuma, Arizona, can legally be given castor oil as punishment – I guess that's what you call having a run for your money!

A self-appointed court of elderly Alaskan Indians on Prince of Wales Island, Alaska, has sentenced two seventeen-year-old boys to, 'Banishment in isolation on two separate uninhabited islands'. The youths were sent to Alaska by a Washington judge who decided they should face tribal – rather than US – justice for stealing $40 from a pizza delivery man. According to people who attended the trial, the judges were somewhat vague – one of the elders wanted to know what kind of topping was on the pizza.

CHAPTER 9

Keep Taking The Tablets

It is illegal to buy ice cream after six p.m. in Newark, New Jersey, unless it is prescribed by a doctor.

A doctor's prescription is needed to bathe in Virginia or Boston.

Troutcreek, Utah, prohibits pharmacists from selling gunpowder to customers for use as a headache remedy. They probably heard that the effects were mind-blowing.

The pharmacy world has advanced quite a bit in the last few centuries. Treatment for nightmares as late as 1850 was a concoction of usnea and pieces of mummy. What's usnea? A moss scraped from a criminal's skull – the worse the crime, the more potent the drug was believed to be. Citizens of eighteenth-century England also believed they could enhance their fortunes by adding the bones of executed criminals to their soup.

In the United States there is a government exhibit of confiscated drugs, devices and food fad items labelled as 'quackery', all of which were found to be completely useless. Amongst the items confiscated from their inventors are:

- A gadget claimed by a salesman to 'remove cobwebs from the brain and rejuvenate the personality glands'.
- A heavy black box called a reflexophone, which was supposed to cure everything – but is completely empty inside.
- Breast enlargers – which we are assured were tested and did not work.
- The Commander, which consists of three rubber rings of various sizes, a plastic applicator ring and a rubber band. The rubber ring is placed on the male organ with the applicator, and the pressure of the rings restricts blood supply and enables the male user to achieve and maintain an erection indefinitely.
- SoloramaBoards, a high-frequency energy generator which, by Thermal Electron Emission, was supposed to relieve pain; cure ruptured discs, breast cancer, bedsores, brain tumours, arthritis and paralysis; heal surgery wounds thirty per cent faster; speed up bone mending; reduce the effects of ageing; relax tension and improve the nerves; cause the rejection of the cancer virus and supply a vital life-force that supports all living matter.

In South Foster, Rhode Island, if a dentist accidentally removed the wrong tooth from a patient the village blacksmith was authorized to remove the corresponding tooth from the dentist. Heavy-handed dentists from Georgia fare little better these days, since it is a misdemeanour if a dentist there is found guilty of cruelty.

A woman can wear false teeth in Vermont only if she has her husband's written permission.

New Orleans edicts declare that biting someone is a 'simple assault' unless you have false teeth, then it is 'aggravated assault'.

In Yukon, Oklahoma, it is illegal for a patient to pull out a dentist's teeth.

CHAPTER 10

Trendy, But Illegal

Surprisingly, hats have been considered by lawmakers through the ages to be an item of clothing which required legal restrictions. In New Jersey there is a law governing millinery which the Ascot authorities may be interested in copying:'Any person who shall wear in a public place any device or thing attached to her head, hair, headgear or hat, which device or thing is capable of lacerating the flesh of any other person with whom it may come in contact and which is not sufficiently guarded against the possibility of so doing, shall be adjudged a disorderly person.'

In Owensboro, Kentucky, if a woman wants to buy a new hat, her husband must try it on first.

When, in 1797, James Heatherington appeared in London wearing the first top hat, he was brought before the Lord Mayor, who bound him over and fined him £50 for, 'appearing on the public highway, wearing upon his head a tall structure, having a shining lustre and calculated to frighten timid people.'

It was illegal in fourteenth-century England for a man to wear a silk nightcap if he earned less than £20 per annum. In Boston, a man must not sleep in day clothing, whatever his income.

In Saco, Missouri, women are prohibited from wearing hats that might frighten timid persons, children or animals.

In Massachusetts it's illegal to wear a turkey feather in your hat.

In Madagascar it is illegal for pregnant women to wear hats or eat eels. What happens if they do both at the same time?

Madonna would do well to avoid Charlotte, North Carolina, when planning her next concert tour. The law there states that all females must at all times have their body covered by a minimum of sixteen yards of cloth. She should also leave Helena, Montana, off her schedule, since women performing in taverns or nightclubs there must wear, 'no less than three pounds 2 ounces of clothing'.

In Hawaii, of all places, it is against the law to be dressed in swimming trunks in public. No comment.

Indecisive ladies beware! Do not shop in Joliet, Illinois, where you will be breaking the law if you try on more than six dresses in one shop.

In St Louis, Missouri, women must be fully dressed, and not be wearing a nightgown, before they can be rescued by a firefighter.

It is a misdemeanour in Schulter, Oklahoma, for a woman to participate in any form of gambling or game of chance while in the nude; while dressed in revealing and sheer clothing; or while wrapped in a towel.

A man wearing a strapless gown in public is breaking the law in Miami, Florida, while in Silver City, New Mexico, it illegal for a woman to dress partly or entirely as a man. Durango, Colorado, is more discerning when it comes to dress sense, with a law that states: 'No man or woman can go to a public place attired in clothing unbecoming to his or her sex.' So if you're a guy who looks great in a strapless but lives in Miami, or a woman whose chicly mannish style annoys the citizenry of Silver City, welcome to Durango!

In 1925 the Greek dictator, General Theodore Pangalos, decreed that no woman could wear a dress with a hemline more than fourteen inches above the ground. It is said he introduced this law because his wife had bow legs!

In 1909 Annette Kellerman wore the first swimsuit, which featured trousers that ended fifty centimetres above the knee and sleeves covering the shoulders. She was arrested for indecent exposure.

It is against the law to wear white shoes in Tibet.

In Norfolk, Virginia, it is illegal for a woman to go to a public dance *without* wearing a corset. However, she cannot make adjustments to her corset while dancing, or even while in the dance hall. The proprietor can have his licence revoked for permitting such wanton activities.

In Sarasota, Florida, it is illegal to sing in public while wearing a swimsuit or bikini.

During the reign of Elizabeth I a law declared that any woman who led a man into marriage through the use of false hair, make-up, false hips, high-heeled shoes or other devices, should be punished with the penalties for witchcraft.

In Minnesota residents may not put male and female underwear next to each other on the clothes line.

Women in Iowa are forbidden to wear corsets. Corset inspectors used to be employed to poke women in the ribs to see if they were wearing them. Perhaps they were the original undercover agents!

During the reign of Emperor Joseph of Austria, nuns were forbidden to wear corsets.

In Maine it is illegal to walk down the streets of any town or city if your shoelaces are not properly tied, and no spiked shoes may be worn in public.

According to the statutes in Providence, Rhode Island, women wearing nylon stockings in public are nothing more than outlaws; while in Bristol, Tennessee, women can wear nylons publicly but they too will be considered common criminals if they stop on the street and adjust, straighten or pull up their hosiery.

In California it is illegal for a woman to drive in her dressing gown.

In St Croix, Wisconsin, it is illegal for a woman to wear red in public while in Minneapolis a woman can wear red whenever she likes – but everyone is prohibited from driving a red car.

In the sixteenth and seventeenth centuries, there was a trend among Venetian prostitutes for high heels. It seems that the higher the women's heels, the more a customer would pay for their services. The fashion was taken to absurd lengths (or rather heights!) and when women began to fall to their deaths by tripping at night into the canals, the city officials enacted a law banning high heels altogether.

In Austin, Texas, it is necessary to purchase a special five-dollar licence in order to walk barefoot on city streets.

It is illegal for women to wear patent leather shoes in public in Cleveland, Ohio. The law states that men might look down and see the reflection of the woman's legs in their shoes.

During the reign of Henry VIII, a law was passed by Parliament limiting the width of a shoe to six inches.

In South Carolina it is illegal to have hip pockets.

New York is a city were the most fashionable 'dress up' each night . . . even the dummies. In fact, it's the law. In the Big Apple, it is illegal to leave a naked dummy in a shop window overnight – they can be naked all day, but you have to dress them up at night.

Louis XVI passed a law stating that everywhere in France the length of the handkerchief had to equal its width.

Oxford, Ohio, has declared it illegal for a woman to strip off her clothing while standing in front of a man's picture.

In Carmel, California, it is illegal for a man to go out wearing a jacket and trousers that do not match.

In 1812, a law was introduced in Sheffield, South Yorkshire, declaring that: 'Under no circumstances whatever shall any preacher who wears trousers be allowed to occupy the pulpit.'

It is illegal to copy the make-up used in the original Frankenstein movie.

In Natoma, Kansas, wearing a striped suit could avert a potentially life-threatening situation, as it is illegal to practise knife-throwing at someone wearing such a garment.

CHAPTER 11

Blame The Parents

In Sweden it is illegal for parents to insult their children. What about a law about children insulting parents?

Adolescent tantrums were rarely seen in seventeenth-century Connecticut, where people could receive the death penalty for disobeying a parent. Tell that to the Swedes.

Omaha, Nebraska: A parent can be arrested if his or her child burps in church.

In Hengelo, the Netherlands, a man who was caught shop-lifting nappies panicked and fled the supermarket, leaving his baby behind. He was identified and arrested when the baby's mother came to fetch their abandoned child.

What's in a name? Inquire of the French where the process of naming a child is taken very seriously. French parents can face arrest for naming baby girls Prune, Cherry or Vanilla.

In the Malagasay Indian tribes it is against the law for a son to be taller than his father. If he is, it costs him either money or an ox.

Boston decrees it is illegal to bathe children on Sundays. Apparently cleanliness is not necessarily close to Godliness.

Two babies cannot be in the same bath at the same time in Los Angeles. From what we've heard, the law does not apply to adults!

In Rochester, New York, children cannot walk a tightrope or collect cigar butts.

In Roderfield, West Virginia, only babies are allowed to ride in prams. Surprise, surprise!

Children making faces at other kids during a lesson in Atlanta, Georgia, can be sent to jail.

Hanford, California, has an ordinance preventing anyone trying to stop a child from jumping over puddles.

Boys are not allowed to throw snowballs at trees in Mount Pulaski, Illinois. Oklahoma City and Watertown, New York, legislate that nobody can throw snowballs at anything, ever.

Marbles, that apparently harmless pastime of many small boys, has been the subject of much discussion in state legislatures in America. In Ashland, Wisconsin, it is against the law to play marbles for keeps and in Charlestown marble playing is illegal on Sunday. Most devastating of all, however, is a law passed in McPherson, Kansas, where it is illegal for small boys to play marbles at all.

Bruce Janu, a high school teacher in Chicago, seems to have found the answer to disciplinary problems. Culprits are put in detention and forced to listen to his extensive collection of Frank Sinatra records. 'The kids just hate it,' he says. 'They're so miserable. And nobody ever comes in just to listen to the music.' When asked about this punishment by irate parents, Mr Janu may be expected to say 'I do it *my way*'.

Singaporeans who refuse to help support their aged and poor parents may be fined or jailed under a proposal to enforce filial piety.

CHAPTER 12

That's Entertainment

In Egypt belly dancers can only perform in public if their navels are covered in gauze.

In North Carolina it is illegal to sing out of tune.

In the early 1900s, the *Des Moines Register* newspaper was sued for libel by the Cherry Sisters, an Iowa singing group who had been greatly offended by the paper's review of their act which read: 'Their long skinny arms, equipped with talons at the extremities, swung mechanically, and anon waved frantically at the suffering audience. The mouths of their rancid features opened like caverns, and sounds like the wailings of damned souls issued therefrom.' The judge ordered that the only way to make a fair judgement was to watch their act – he did so and ruled in favour of the paper.

Female tightrope walkers have a hard time of it in Winchester, Massachusetts. The law there states that a young lady cannot be employed to dance on a tightrope, except in church.

Indian filmmakers have to abide by a judgement of the censors regarding the use of the word 'sexy'. It states that the word can only be used in the right context. It is fine to say: 'My pants are sexy. My shirt is also sexy', but it is not possible to say: 'Your mummy is sexy. Your daddy is also sexy'.

In West Bengal, India, it is illegal to play movies showing the act of kissing, nor can films with kissing scenes be made in that area. The Minister of Education said: 'It might cause grave harm to society, as they would act as a brain softener.'

The law prohibits unrestrained giggling in Helena, Montana. Perhaps Noel Britten should consider moving there, to ensure no one breaks the law. He is a tour guide in Bath, Avon, who takes tourists on a 'Bizarre Bath' comedy tour of the town. Mr Britten stops outside certain houses and delivers his jokes about the town's heritage and its famous residents. But the people of Bath are sick of hearing him tell the same old jokes. They have threatened to invoke a 1760 law prohibiting 'noisy activities' if he doesn't improve his act.

In New Jersey, it was for many years against the law to use 'x-ray opera glasses'.

In Salt Lake City, Utah, it is against the law to carry an unwrapped ukelele on the street.

The California Board of Equalization has ruled that bartenders cannot be held culpable for misjudging the age of midgets.

In 1926 the Broadway producer Earl Carroll fell foul of the American prohibition laws when he hosted an orgy at his theatre after a performance of his play *Vanities*. The party was in honour of Countess Vera Cathcart who had just beaten an Immigration Service effort to prevent her from remaining in the country on the grounds of moral turpitude following her sensational divorce from the Earl of Cathcart. At the climax of the evening's entertainment, a bathtub on the stage was filled with champagne and a nude model climbed in while men eagerly waited to fill their glasses. When Carroll was hauled before a federal grand jury to explain his violation of the prohibition laws, he declared there was no champagne in the bathtub, merely ginger ale. Unfortunately the jury did not believe him and he was convicted of perjury, fined $2,000 and sent to prison for a year and a day. (He was released after serving four months.)

It is illegal to play the fiddle in Boston.

In Gary, Indiana, it is illegal to go to the theatre within four hours of eating garlic.

In Bellingham, Washington, a woman may not take more than three steps backward while dancing.

Don't dance too close in Utah – daylight must be visible between dancing partners.

In Boston night clubs, it is against the law to hold frog-jumping competitions.

The military governor of Chile issued the following decree: 'It is more worthwhile to admire a good landscape than a photograph of a nude woman.'

New York cinema owners must scrape chewing gum from under their seats every month.

In Iowa the law states: 'a one-armed piano player may be seen, but not if admission is charged to view his performance.'

In Star, Mississippi, it is illegal to ridicule public architecture.

In Winnetka, Illinois you cannot take your shoes off in a movie theatre if your feet smell. *Now that's one law most people would approve of!*

CHAPTER 13

Going Off The Rails

A sign on a railway track in Korea reads: 'Positively No Intercourse on These Tracks While Trains Are Passing'.

The train system in Kansas must carry a great many short loads. The law there states: 'the last car must be left off all trains running within the state of Kansas'.

In 1984, lawyers in India finally succeeded in obtaining bail for a client who had been held in prison for twenty-nine years while awaiting trial. His alleged offence: travelling by train without a ticket! His name came to the attention of prison authorities who could find no record of his conviction or sentence when he was about to be transferred to another prison.

In Kansas there is a law that reads: 'when trains meet at a crossing, both shall come to a full stop and neither shall proceed until the other has gone.'

When SNCF, the French railway, spent hundreds of thousands of pounds launching Eurostar as the name for the train using the Channel Tunnel, they overlooked one thing – a small courier company called Eurostart which been trading for some years. Eurostart claimed that the name was too similar to their own. A Paris court agreed, and ordered the railway to change their name within six months or pay a fine of £120 every time the name is used.

Carolina has its own form of prohibition. It is illegal to drink milk in a train passing through North Carolina. There's no word on the status of bourbon – so have a good journey!

Guess who's coming for dinner. Railway engineers in North Dakota are not allowed to take their trains home with them – unless they carry a full crew.

Following a lengthy dispute, a New York court made the following ruling: 'A railway company which negligently throws a passenger from a crowded car on a trestle is held liable for injury to a relative who, in going to his rescue, falls through the trestle.' Suddenly, leaves on the line seem less irritating.

CHAPTER 14

Politicians Know Best

A bill has been passed in California to repeal a number of old and useless laws – it is entitled the JUNK bill which stands for Jurassic, Unproductive, Negligible and Knucklehead laws. Amongst the laws to be repealed are those involving dead-or-alive rewards and duelling. There were also laws still on the books prohibiting horses from mating in public – they had to be in enclosures so they could not be seen by innocent passers-by – and laws specifying damages for seduction.

In Ancient Egypt a tax collector found guilty of stealing from poor people had his nose cut off.

The North Yemen government decreed the following: 'All official titles used in correspondence addresses, mass media and in various official quarters will be completely abolished, to be replaced by the word "brother" at all levels.' The decree was signed, 'Lieutenant Colonel Ibahim Hamadi, Chairman of the Command Council and Commander in Chief of the Armed Forces'. What's good for the goose is not necessarily good for the gander.

66

A Saigon policeman was cited for honesty in 1970. Apparently the young officer was offered a $10 bribe, which he refused. The South Vietnamese Government was so impressed they awarded him a medal.

In Minnesota, the law states that taxpayers must include on their return their 'name, address, Social Security number, age, date of birth, date of death'. As the saying goes, you can avoid anything except death and taxes.

On the USA Tax form 1040 one of the categories of income which the government states must be declared is 'embezzled or other illegal income'.

When John F Kennedy was assassinated in 1963 it was not a federal crime to kill a President of the United States.

Some recently proposed laws in the US:

- Armless motorists should be exempt from paying tolls on the New Jersey Turnpike.
- West Virginia marriage licences should include a warning that domestic violence is a crime.
- Gambling on rubber duck races should be allowed in Nebraska.
- In Nevada, real estate agents should be protected from lawsuits for failing to tell buyers that someone had died of natural causes in a house.
- Tripping a horse on purpose in California should be punishable by a fine and possible jail sentence.

The US Department of the Treasury has a very unusual office, where the 'Conscience Fund' is kept. Every morning, a mailbag is picked up containing monies that are voluntarily given back to the government. The Conscience Fund was established in 1811 to accept an anonymous donation of five dollars from a person claiming to have defrauded the government. Since then, millions of dollars have been returned. Monies received are usually in small amounts – from a postage stamp up – although occasional deposits of several thousand dollars are received. The largest single deposit was $139,000.

The fund gets most of its contributions from citizens who cheated on their income taxes. They went undetected by Internal Revenue Service auditors, but could not escape their own consciences. Other conscience-stricken contributors stole government property while in military service. Contributors usually wish to remain anonymous, but one, who signed himself John Doe, put a toe print on his form for proof of identification in case of an IRS audit.

The letters that are sent to the Conscience Fund would make interesting reading for a psychologist studying guilt. Here's a random selection:

- 'Please accept this money enclosed for two postal stamps I re-used.'
- 'This check for $1,300 is to make restitution of tools, leave days, and other things I stole while I was in the Navy from 62–67.'
- 'If I am to be prosecuted for this, you can get my address off the check.'
- 'Two years ago I brought a ring into this country from abroad and did not declare it. This $50 will more than cover the amount. Thank you.'
- 'Enclosed is $210 for some letters I read many years ago and some food I didn't pay for.'

A Virginia statute is entitled: 'To Prohibit Corrupt Practices or Bribery by Any Person Other than Candidates'.

There is a Missouri law entitled: 'Senate Substitute for Senate Committee Substitute for House Substitute for House Committee Substitute for House Bill 6579'. Who says politicians don't know what they're talking about?

CHAPTER 15

Of Mice And Men

Being able to tell the time is a prerequisite for a dog in Smithtown, New York, where canines are prohibited from barking for more than fifteen minutes at a time.

A dog is not always a man's best friend – particularly when his master happens to be a thief. In Osaka, Japan, a man tied his dog to a railing as he tried to break into a house. The thief was disturbed and fled, leaving his dog – Lucky – tied to the railing. The police arrived and untied Lucky, who led them straight to his master's house. As the man was arrested, one of the police officers commented, 'If I was that dog, I would start thinking about moving to another town'.

In International Falls, Minnesota, cats cannot chase dogs up telephone poles.

In Normal, Oklahoma, it is illegal to make ugly faces at a dog – violators can be arrested and fined. It's just not considered *Normal* behaviour!

In Hartford, Connecticut, attempting to teach or try to educate a dog is illegal.

A miniature schnauzer puppy was stolen by mistake in London when the handbag it was sleeping inside was snatched in Oxford Street. It was eventually reunited with its distraught owner, still dressed in the yellow jumper and Barbour style jacket it was wearing when it was stolen.

Marco el Narco, a Belgian Shepherd, is a police dog with a difference. Marvellous Marco is a supersniffer who so far has sniffed out ten tonnes of marijuana, 500 kilograms of cocaine, and eight kilograms of heroin along the highways of Mexico. In fact, he has proved so successful at sniffing out drugs that traffickers have decided to hit back: wanted posters have appeared promising a $25,000 reward for his pelt. In order to prevent any harm coming to the wonder dog, his trainer sleeps with him and he is given only American dog food to eat.

In Shawnee, Oklahoma, three or more dogs must have written permission to meet together on private property. This must be to discourage clandestine canine bridge or poker games.

Sleeping in a dog kennel is illegal in Wallace, Idaho. For humans, that is!

In Zion, Illinois, it is illegal to give lighted cigars to dogs, cats or other domesticated animals kept as pets.

71

A warning to all dog owners. Putting up a 'Beware of the Dog' sign could get you into deeper trouble if your dog actually bites someone. If the victim can prove that the owner knew his dog was vicious, it is much easier to collect damages. So if your dog bites, beware of the beware of the dog signs.

In Winchester, Hampshire, a postman was jailed for nine months after he admitted mailing pornographic material to people whose dogs barked at him. Alan Fenney posted marital aids such as vibrators through the letterboxes of those house-holders with angry dogs. He also admitted sending sexual material to dignitaries and people with titles because of his personal objections to Britain's honours system.

Beavers in Connecticut are legally entitled to build a dam, while sheep in Los Angeles are allowed to graze on Baldwin Hill – as long as they leave two inches of grass. So if you see a sheep carrying a tape measure, you'll know he's from LA!

In Baltimore, Maryland, it is against the law to mistreat an oyster and in Topeka, Kansas, it is illegal to worry a squirrel. But the law in San Antonio, Texas, is tougher on some animals – there it is illegal for monkeys to ride on buses.

A California woman was devastated at the loss of her dog, and offered a $2,500 reward for the return of her pet. Some time later, a couple arrived carrying the bones of a dog which they claimed was hers. The woman refused to pay the reward, and the couple sued. The judge found for the owner.

State law in Arkansas prohibits the blindfolding of cows on public highways.

In Klamath Falls, Oregon, it is illegal to kick the heads off snakes.

For years, cotton farmers in North Carolina have been seriously handicapped by a law stating that they cannot use elephants for ploughing or planting cotton.

Bankrupt property developer Malcolm Kellar is on the run, leaving behind an unfinished mansion and £6 million in debts. There is a reward of £100,000 for finding him. The police thought tracking him down would be no problem, since he was travelling with a one-legged toucan – who has a wooden leg – a pet lynx, llamas and several peacocks. Two years after his mysterious disappearance, however, he and his menagerie are still on the loose.

Between 1 March and 20 October, Residents of Nottingham, Maryland, must let their hogs roam free.

Rabbits seem to have caused problems throughout America, where it has been considered necessary to introduce some stringent laws. In Tuscumbia, Alabama, for instance, it is illegal for more than eight rabbits to live on the same block. In New York State it is illegal to shoot at a rabbit from a moving trolley car. Please get off the car, or wait for it to come to a complete stop, then fire away!

The cartoon character Donald Duck was banned in Finland because he didn't wear trousers.

In Ottawa, Canada, there is a stinger of an anti-noise law which prohibits the buzzing of bees. No one is quite sure how the law should be enforced, since the bees seem to ignore the posted signs, they don't quite fit into the standard handcuffs, and no police officers are willing to serve a warrant. Rumours buzzing around the local station are that the bees attack the long arm of the law whenever it reaches out for them.

It is against the law to carry bees in your hat in Lawrence, Kansas. Could this be the origin of having a bee in one's bonnet?

In Alaska it's fine to hunt a bear as long as you're licensed to do so, but illegal to 'disturb a grizzly bear in order to take its picture'.

A hunter from outside the tribe would be in serious trouble among the Ba-ila people of central Africa if, after killing an elephant, he walked around the back of the animal or laughed at its buttocks.

Imitating animals is illegal in Miami.

In Pacific Grove, California, it is a misdemeanour to kill or threaten a butterfly.

In Florida two men have been prosecuted for cattle rustling after DNA taken from a calf matched the DNA taken from an uncooked slab of pot roast sold by the men. Seems the pot roast was formerly the calf's mother.

In Fairbanks, Alaska, it is illegal to feed any kind of alcoholic beverage, beer or wine, to a moose. Moreover, moose are banned from walking on the pavements of Fairbanks even if they *are* sober. It is illegal to look at a moose from the window of an aeroplane or any other flying vehicle anywhere in Alaska.

In Natchez, Mississippi, it is illegal for an elephant to guzzle beer while in Oklahoma it is illegal to get a fish drunk. Before you know it they'll be exhibiting anti-social behaviour, dropping out of school . . .

If you are in Seattle and decide to take your goldfish for a ride on a bus – beware. You are only permitted to do so if they lie absolutely still.

In Denver, Colorado you can go to jail for mistreating a rat. Only the animal kind.

It used to be illegal to own a dog taller than ten inches in height in Boston, Massachusetts.

In Jefferson City, Missouri, no farmer can ride an ox down the street in a violent manner.

Riding a horse in a saloon is illegal in Ellensburg, Washington, Prescott, Arizona, and the state of California. If your horse really needs a drink, saloons in Burns, Oregon, are accommodating, provided you pay a fee.

It is illegal for a donkey to sleep in a bath in Brooklyn, New York.

Why did the chicken cross the road? In Quitman, Georgia, it could only be because he wanted to spend the night in prison – it is illegal for a chicken to cross the road there.

In Marblehead, Massachusetts, while a chicken may cross the road on a Sunday, a person cannot unless he can prove it is absolutely necessary, or perhaps if he is holding a chicken!

It is illegal to pick feathers from a live goose in California.

Policemen in Paulding, Ohio, are permitted to bite a barking dog in order to quieten him down, but they had better not get into a fight with a bull in Washington DC where it's illegal to punch a bull on the nose.

If you kill an animal with malicious intent in Oklahoma, you could be charged with first degree murder.

Riding an ugly horse in Wilbur, Washington, will land the horseman a $300 fine.

In South Carolina it's a crime to perform dental work on a mule or horse to conceal the animal's age. You can, however, turn back their odometers.

In Berea, Kentucky, it is illegal to take a horse out at night on the streets and highways unless a red tail-light is attached to its rear. In Ohio, *all* domestic animals must wear tail-lights outdoors.

In Norfolk, Virginia, hens are banned from laying eggs before eight a.m. and after four p.m. If a hen breaks the law, maybe they send Marmite soldiers to arrest her.

In Essex Falls, New Jersey, ducks cannot quack after ten while in Memphis, Tennessee, croaking frogs must silence themselves by eleven p.m.

In Baltimore, Maryland, it's unlawful to give a parrot away, but it's fine to take a lion to the movies.

Lawbooks in Fountain Inn, South Carolina, state that horses must wear pants; in Charleston, Virginia, nappies are required if the horse is pulling a carriage. Breaking the law results in a fine or jail term, presumably for the driver. You can also find horses in nappies in parts of Oregon, Tennessee, and Georgia. If you're looking, that is.

In Clawson City, Michigan, the law books state that it is perfectly legal for people to sleep with their pigs, cows and chickens. The jury is still out regarding elephants and llamas.

Non-US citizens cannot let their goats run loose in West Virginia, although it is fine if you are an American.

Ohio speed laws state: 'A jackass cannot be ridden faster than six m.p.h. . . .'

It is illegal to hunt camels in the state of Arizona.

It is illegal to own a dog in Reykjavík, Iceland.

An old Hollywood bylaw forbids driving more than 2,000 sheep down Hollywood Boulevard at once.

In Maine it is illegal to set your mule on fire.

If you happen to pass by a cow in the Pine Island district of Minnesota, remember your manners – a man must tip his hat when doing so.

This one's pretty obvious really – in Michigan you may not tie a crocodile up to a fire hydrant.

Painting a horse is illegal in Vermont.

Until this century, dachshunds could not be kept as pets in Massachusetts.

CHAPTER 16

Kangaroo Court – Animals In The Dock

When a thirty-year-old woman from Wisconsin was found crushed to death in 1982, Anna Mae was arrested on suspicion of murder. Anna Mae's footprints were taken, and she was found to be the culprit. She was later released, but her handlers were charged with murder. Anna Mae was a five-tonne circus elephant.

In England and Europe during the Middle Ages it was illegal for any animal to injure or kill a human being. It was even common practice to try to condemn animals for their illicit behaviour! In one documented case, the French parliament, the highest court in the nation, ordered the execution of a cow. It was hanged and then burned at the stake. Or should we say steak!

In 1386 at Falaise, a judge ordered a pig to have its legs mutilated and then be hanged for killing a child. The pig was dressed in the child's jacket and taken to the town square for the public execution.

At Lavegny in France in 1457, a sow and her six piglets were tried for the murder of a child who, it was claimed, they had killed and eaten. The sow was found guilty and condemned to death, but the piglets were acquitted because they were considered too young to know what they were doing.

In 1576 in Schweinfurt, Germany, a hasty executioner killed a pig accused of murder. As the trial had not yet taken place, the pig was not proven guilty, so the executioner was chased out of town by an angry and indignant mob.

Bartholomew Chassenée, a French lawyer, was appointed by the court to represent a group of defendants who had no lawyer of their own. The defendants in question were rats. And, as it turned out, their lawyer performed admirably. The rats were accused of destroying crops on a number of local farms. First, Chassenée declared that the trial could not begin because the summons had not been served correctly, and not all his clients had actually received the summons. The court reluctantly agreed, and subsequently the summons was read publicly in all the churches of the parishes where the accused rats lived. Chassenée then declared that the trial could not continue because his clients were in danger of losing their lives on the way to the court, as they might be eaten by cats. Chassenée must have impressed the court, as he was later made a judge and, in fact, used the case of the rats to prove that heretics should be allowed legal representation, reasoning that if rats were entitled to legal representation then so were any humans.

Another case where an animal was acquitted took place in 1750, also in France, when a man and a mare were accused jointly of bestiality. The man was found guilty and executed, but the mare was acquitted on the grounds that she had not consented to the act. Well, she would say that, wouldn't she?

In 1587, worms were put on trial in Bordeaux – but the outcome of the trial will never be known because the last page of the trial transcript was destroyed – it was eaten by worms.

Because they were destroying the food and furniture of the monastery, Brazilian monks sued some termites in 1713. The termites were represented by a good lawyer who pointed out that the termites had been there first. He added that the termites were much more industrious and productive than the monks. Clearly the court had some sympathy with this argument, and ordered that the termites remove themselves to another area, where they could continue to live and work undisturbed. It was reported at the time that the termites complied with the order and marched out of the monastery to their new home.

The last trial of an animal was in 1740 in France, when a cow was found guilty of witchcraft and hanged.

Animals have been lynched in the US – on 13 September, 1916, Mary, a circus elephant that had killed three men was hanged in Erwin, Tennessee.

A crow was arrested in Japan for pecking children and using obscene language. To compound his crime, the crow refused to answer questions at the local police station in Myzaki City. He was eventually released, and subsequently appeared on Japanese television. There was some mention of him having his own talk show . . .

A man from Pasadena shot his parrot dead because he claimed the parrot was laughing at him while he was arguing with his mother.

Monkeys are quite safe in South Bend, Indiana – as long as they are non-smokers. A monkey was tried and convicted there for smoking a cigarette.

A racoon called Jasper is the only member of his species ever to appear as a plaintiff in a legal claim. Jasper's tail was cut off by a train when he crossed a railroad track on his way to start his winter hibernation. His master claimed damages but lost the case.

The United States Government once took action against some cartons of tinned sardines in Western Pennsylvania. It was claimed that the cartons had been improperly marked. The sardines were found guilty, but the foreman of the jury recommended that the court have mercy. Judge Gibson, who presided over the fishy trial, agreed to consider the recommendation.

CHAPTER 17

Death Is No Excuse

Anyone contemplating suicide in England before 1961 had more to worry about than leaving their affairs in order and ensuring that the method chosen was effective and painless. If the suicide attempt failed, the unfortunate survivor would be subject to criminal prosecution and punishment. In some cases the penalty was death. Until 1823, even a successful suicide was penalised. In order not to cheat the death penalty which would have been invoked for a failed suicide, a stake would be driven through the body of the unfortunate soul before it was buried in unconsecrated ground at the side of a road.

A man from West Germany made twenty-eight unsuccessful suicide bids. He slashed his wrists ten times, took poison four times and tried to hang himself twice, he also tried stabbing, gas, drowning, drug overdose and throwing himself under a moving vehicle. On his final attempt, upon finding his wife in bed with her lover, he dragged her from her bed and holding her jumped backwards from a window. Unfortunately she hit the ground first and he landed on top of her. She died. He is still alive, and serving a sentence for manslaughter.

Although sentenced to be hanged for murder, William Kogut, known in San Quentin as convict number 1651, swore he would kill himself rather than give the state the pleasure of executing him. Kogut was kept under constant surveillance to prevent any possibility of suicide.

During the autumn of 1930, Kogut spent the bulk of his time playing solitaire. Night after night he tore out the red heart and diamond shapes from each card, storing them in a hollow leg in his bunk. On the night of 9 October, 1930, Kogut took the leg, filled it with water, sealed both ends and placed it on a heater in his cell. Several hours later this makeshift pipe bomb, the cell, and Kogut blew up. What he knew, and his careless caretakers did not, was that the ink forming the red symbols on the playing cards contained nitrate and cellulose, an explosive mixture when combined with water. Kogut may have cheated the authorities when he dealt his last card, but he did not cheat death.

On the ancient Greek island of Delos, it was illegal to be born or to die.

A law worth remembering if you visit New York — it is a misdemeanour to arrest a dead man for debt.

Convicted murderer Michael Godwin received a last minute reprieve from the electric chair when his death sentence was commuted to life imprisonment. Several weeks later, Godwin was trying to fix the electrical cord from the TV set in his new cell. For reasons known only to Godwin, he bit into the cord, while sitting on the metal frame of his bed. In a shocking twist of fate, he electrocuted himself by gnawing on the exposed wire.

The name of Poor John Lacy is indelibly linked to the infamous Halifax Gibbet, a forerunner of the guillotine built in 1286. For hundreds of years the law stated that if any condemned criminal could withdraw his head from the gibbet between the time the blade was released and the time it hit the bottom, then run to the nearby town of Hebblebrook before being caught, he would be set free, unconditionally. The only man to challenge the Halifax Gibbet successfully and run to Hebblebrook, and freedom, was John Lacy.

Why, then, 'Poor John Lacy'? For seven years he boasted about his miraculous deed. He went on for so long that people got sick of hearing about it. Eventually they stopped believing him altogether.

Lacy had difficulty dealing with the sceptics, so he decided he was going to have to prove what he had done. What better way to do so than by doing it again. He made his way back to Halifax and placed his neck in the gibbet. He smiled at the disbelievers and the blade was set free. You can probably guess the rest about Poor John Lacy.

As for the Halifax Gibbet, it can still be seen, just as it was during the days of its use. It was taken out of commission in 1650, but its ability to attract curious sightseers is still very much alive.

If you were condemned to be beheaded in England, you were advised to tip the executioner generously. If the executioner felt sympathetically inclined towards his victim, he would sharpen the blade, and ensure that the job was completed in one blow. Poor Mary Queen of Scots must have been a bad tipper – it took fifteen blows of the axe to remove her head.

The most severe penalty used during the Yüan dynasty in China was death by slow slicing.

One of the earliest cases where a condemned person survived the hangman in England was that of Inetta de Balsham who had been convicted and condemned to death for harbouring thieves during the time of King Henry III. The woman was hanged on a Monday at nine a.m. and continued to hang until the following Thursday when she was found to be still alive. It was discovered that de Balsham's windpipe was deformed and had ossified so that the rope failed to cut off her ability to breathe. King Henry was so amazed at her remarkable survival that she was pardoned.

According to official figures, fifty-eight people died in California's January 1994 earthquake. In the six months following the quake, however, there have been over 400 requests for the $6,000 burial grant from federal disaster funds.

When Reverend Dr Dodd, an eighteenth-century forger, was sentenced to death by hanging for his crimes, he made a speech showing such piety and remorse that he aroused a huge amount of sympathy amongst the public, many of whom decided this man should not die. A plan was formulated to rush him to a waiting doctor at the expiration of the legal minimum period of suspension. However, because of the warmth of feeling towards the good doctor, the crowd witnessing the event was so huge that his friends could not carry his body through quickly enough to save his live. Dr Dodd's popularity turned out to be the death of him.

Will Purvis was found guilty of the murder of a Mississippi farmer. He insisted he was innocent and his friends came to his defence. They knew Will Purvis to be a man of his word. Apparently, this wasn't enough to sway the jury. After the guilty verdict had been delivered, Purvis proclaimed to the members of the jury: 'I'll live to see every last one of you die!' And, being a man of his word, he meant it!

Nobody in town took the condemned man seriously. After all, he was justifiably upset about his imminent execution. The date for the hanging was set and the gallows were built. Eventually, the noose was placed around Purvis's neck. As the trap doors flung open, Purvis plunged to purgatory . . . or so everyone thought.

It seems that the noose was loose. It slipped over Purvis's neck and he fell to the ground with a crash. The sheriff was willing to give it another try, but the spectators on hand got out of control. They thought it was a miracle and that Purvis should be set free.

The sheriff, not wanting to lose his own neck, took Purvis back to his cell where he waited until things simmered down. Before a new date could be set, some of Purvis's friends smuggled him out of jail and into hiding. Once again, he had eluded death.

Finally, after thousands of letters pleading for clemency poured into the governor's office, Purvis was pardoned. Many years later, a dying man confessed to the murder for which Will Purvis had been condemned. Purvis had been proved to be a man of his word. As for his last words to the jury that had condemned him? Will Purvis died on October 13, 1938, three days after the death of the last juror who had sentenced him to hang. He had seen every one of them die!

A Nigerian witch doctor faces the death penalty if his bullet-proof charms fail to work.

In France, during the early eighteenth century, the job of Chief Executioner was handed down from father to son. So when Charles-Jean-Baptiste Sanson died in 1726 his son Charles automatically assumed the role of executioner – even though he was only seven years old.

As Charles was not strong enough to decapitate the condemned prisoners himself, he was permitted to employ a helper named Prudhomme who actually wielded the heavy executioner's sword. Charles had to be present for every execution because he was the only person who was authorized officially to commit the act. He finally took over his official duties as Chief Executioner at the grand old age of twelve.

During the reign of Henry IV, it was illegal for sheriffs to behead someone who was sentenced to hang.

CHAPTER 18

Daylight Robberies

The State of Louisiana declares it wrongful to rob a bank and shoot a bank teller with a water pistol.

Armed police laid siege for over two hours to a TSB bank in the Arndale Centre in Manchester, only to discover that the bank was empty. The gunman had fled without anyone noticing.

In LA two armed robbers burst into a bank and demanded that everyone lie down on the floor. Realizing there was now no one left to gather up the money, the pair hesitated, then fled in panic.

In County Mayo, Ireland, an unidentified man succeeded in exchanging a wad of children's play money for £100. The culprit convinced the foreign exchange teller that the toy money was legal Peruvian tender. Unconfirmed reports say that the police are currently interrogating a suspect with big ears, believed to be from Toytown . . .

Mark McKenna admitted in London's Central Criminal Court that he tried to rob a betting shop by sticking his fingers under his sweater to look like a gun. He was caught when a cashier handed over the money and McKenna absent-mindedly pulled out his hand to take the cash.

A bank robbery in Texas was foiled because the bank was no longer a bank. The bank had closed several months earlier, making way for an insurance office. Lea Ables, who worked in the insurance company described the attempted heist: 'He walked in here and said, "Give me your money", and I laughed. I didn't think he was serious at first. He then sort of looked funny and asked, "This ain't a bank any more?"' The gunman escaped, having first robbed two of the employees of a total of $127.

Boston police were baffled by a series of bank raids carried out in the late 1930s. At the scene of each crime, the thumb print of a well-known gangster called Ben Franklin was found. But Franklin had been dead for several months. One day, acting on a tip-off, the police hid in a bank and waited for the mystery raiders to arrive. The gang entered, filled their bags with money and jewellery, then pulled a human thumb out of a case and left its imprint on the safe door.

In the pre-computer era, it was calculated that there were approximately 200 different ways to embezzle money from a bank without danger of immediate exposure. John Rankine, IBM's director of data security, believes that now, with computers and advanced technology, the ways are too numerous to be counted.

Police in Nairobi had a slightly easier task than their Boston counterparts. They were called to investigate the scene of a burglary in which the thief had left his entire hand behind. The homeowner had caught the burglar and chopped off his hand with a Japanese Samurai sword. The police kept the hand in the mortuary fridge until the owner was found. He was afterwards known as Cool Hand Luke!

When successful counterfeiters Baldwin Bredell and Arthur Taylor were finally caught and sent to prison, they saw no reason to retire from business. With the help of relatives, who smuggled in supplies, they began producing $20 bills from their cells at night. They had a problem finding the correct ink, so they stole bleaches from the prison laundry and dried fruits and berries and green leaves brought to them by relatives and made their own dye. They were eventually caught by Chief John E Wilkie, but no one could believe that such perfect fake bills could be produced without an eight tonne press, a camera and a huge workroom. Only when the two re-enacted their feat were the experts convinced.

In recognition of their extraordinary talents, Chief Wilkie decided to help them get a new start in life when they were released. He got financial backing for a mechanical engraving machine Taylor had perfected, and the ex-counterfeiter became a successful manufacturer. Bredell went on to establish a leading engraving and lithography plant and both became comfortably – and legitimately – wealthy.

In Salt Lake City a would-be robber walked up to a teller asking her to hand over all the money. As she was gathering it up, however, the robber fainted and didn't come to until the police had arrived.

The cashier of an Ohio bank was convicted of embezzling $7,500 over a period of ten years, ending in 1941. During the trial, the judge, Frank L Kloeb, learned that the man had started as a cashier in 1920 at an annual salary of $1,080 per annum and twenty-two years later was earning only $1,900. The cashier had stopped his embezzlements as his salary started to rise faster and was not found out for many years. The judge deferred sentencing indefinitely and refused even to put the cashier on probation. 'If I had the authority,' the judge declared, 'I would sentence the bank officers and the Board of Directors to read the story of Scrooge at Christmas and think of the defendant.'

In Chicago a torch man burned his way into four safes in a row and succeeded in burning the money inside each of them to a crisp. In New Jersey two would-be safe-crackers worked over a safe with acetylene torches for three hours, succeeding in welding it permanently shut.

A thief in Johannesburg got a nasty surprise when he snatched the bulging bag of his victim. All it contained was ten bottles of urine which she was taking to the laboratory for analysis.

A would-be robber entered a store in Riverside, California, aiming to rob one of the cash registers and make his escape. He came prepared with a pillowcase to pull over his head, so no one would be able to identify him. Unfortunately, he forgot to cut eye-holes into the pillowcase and could find neither the cash desk nor the exit from the store. He lifted the bottom of the pillowcase so he could see, and was immediately recognized by one of the customers.

It was during the 1830s that Sile Doty's career as a thief flourished. He became known in America as one of the great lock men of crime and was the first to develop the complete burglar kit. He so loved anything to do with locks that he designed handcuffs which he sold to sheriffs. Fortunately for the criminals he also sold special keys that could open the cuffs while they were worn. Another fine example of good old Yankee ingenuity.

In Queens, New York City, an unemployed shoe salesman walked into a bank and handed a teller a note demanding 'all your tens, twenties and thirties'. When he left, he was followed by a bank officer as he walked to a motel a block away from the scene of the crime. He was arrested by the police within fifteen minutes.

One bank teller became so unnerved while being robbed she put a waste-basket over her head as protection. The shocked bandit ran out of the bank. In another bank a patient robber stood by and watched while the very precise teller counted and recounted the money before handing it over. So did everyone else in the bank. The robber took his money and calmly walked out of bank, knowing exactly what he was getting away with.

CHAPTER 19

Publish And Be Damned

The Bible, thought by many to be the original law book, has occasionally caused a few legal problems. In 1631, an authorized edition of the Bible was printed in London – with an unfortunate misprint. The seventh commandment read 'Thou shalt commit adultery'. It became known as 'The Wicked Bible', and its printers, Robert Barker and Martin Lucas, were fined £3,000.

During the colonial days of America, it wasn't just the authors of offensive books that were punished – the books were too. In a Massachusetts case, a book was sentenced to be publicly whipped with forty stripes and then burnt. In 1754 a hangman was assigned to perform the same task on a pamphlet that criticized the court. The punishment was carried out publicly in Boston's King Street.

British tabloids please note: In Oklahoma it is illegal to print a lie in a newspaper in order to increase sales.

In August 1994 police in Sâo Paulo, Brazil, arrested master thief Robson Augusto Araujo and confiscated a stash of his business cards which bore the company name (in Portuguese) 'Thefts and Robberies Ltd' and gave his job title as 'Thief'. He was caught because although the card's address was, of course, fake, the cellular phone number was real.

You cannot libel the dead, but you can, it seems, be libelled from the grave . . . When H Lawrence Nelson of Raleigh, North Carolina, was killed in 1906, his friends and relatives wanted it to be remembered who was responsible for his death – so they had it inscribed on his tombstone: 'H Lawrence Nelson, born Dec 16 1880. Murdered and robbed by Hamp Kendall, Sept 25 1906'. Kendall had indeed been convicted of the crime, and was sentenced to life imprisonment. Eleven years later, however, the real murderer confessed and Kendall was released from prison. Kendall petitioned the courts to have the offending tombstone altered, but the courts said they had no jurisdiction. After many years of fighting with various authorities, including the church that owned the graveyard, Kendall finally succeeded in convincing the legislature to pass a law declaring illegal 'any tombstone which charges anyone with a crime'. In 1950 the libellous inscription was finally removed – thirty-three years after Kendall was exonerated of having committed the crime.

CHAPTER 20

Courtroom Capers

Butchers were not allowed to serve on juries in medieval Europe as they were considered to be insensitive.

In 1993 British justice was sorely tried by a complex legal conundrum – can a court accept a dog's evidence when the animal cannot be cross-examined by defence lawyers? Eventually, Lord Justice Taylor, the Lord Chief Justice of England, issued a seventeen-page judgement. He ruled that so long as the handler could establish the reliability of the dog and the trial judge warned the jury about the need to examine the dog's evidence with care, the evidence could properly be admitted.

Criminals in Texas must give the intended victim twenty-four hours notice in writing, or orally if possible, of the crime to be committed, and where and when it will take place. If they do not comply, they have broken the law before they have even committed the crime!

Police officers in Key West, Florida, are banned from gossiping while on duty.

New Jersey decrees that it is illegal to frown at a police officer. Smile please, you're under arrest . . .

An enactment in Maine makes it unlawful to arrest a dead man. But if you break this law, it might be worth asking for the case to be heard in Oregon, where it is illegal for a dead juror to serve on a jury.

Lack of personal hygiene in days gone by meant that the close confines of courtrooms were often unbearable, and sometimes even deadly! When a senior judge died in 1849, his passing was attributed to severe exhaustion after enduring the stink of a three-day session at the Old Bailey.

An ex-robber turned lawyer, George Freyn, has devised a course entitled 'How to Make Any Jury Like You', and promises that anyone attending the course will have the twelve jury members eating out their hand. His course in New York includes tips such as: Look pathetic, blame your parents, carry a Bible. If you follow his instructions, he claims: 'You can beat your wife to a pulp, work a savings and loan swindle, even murder your parents or slice off your husband's privates – and not serve one day in prison.' Freyn recently finished serving twelve years for armed robbery.

Hernando Rojas, a sixty-four-year-old Peruvian lawyer, has produced a brochure which includes pictures of himself in various states of undress, posing in his office, on a motorcycle and in court. He says, 'In all of them I am wearing a tie and holding legal documents so customers will know I am a qualified professional.'

As late as the seventeenth century, American colonists employed the medieval custom of trial by touch in murder cases. It was believed that if the accused was the murderer, the corpse would give some signal. In a typical case in Virginia in 1663, several members of a family were accused of killing a former servant. They were all ordered to touch the body, and when it gave no sign, they were found not guilty. However, when Thomas Lutherland was tried for the murder of John Clark in New Jersey in 1691, he was less fortunate. The body was brought into court and Lutherland was ordered to touch it. There was no reaction from the corpse, but there was from the court which decided that Lutherland was guilty anyway, and he was hanged.

CHAPTER 21

Walls Do Not A Prison Make

In ancient Rome if a prisoner escaped from jail, his jailer could be executed.

If a prisoner escapes from jail in Alamos, Mexico, the guard on duty will have to serve out the sentence. Needless to say, Alamos guards take their jobs very seriously.

A Belfast Crown Court judge was reluctant to send burglar Raymond Martin to prison, even though he had pleaded guilty to a string of offences. The problem was, it didn't seem like much of a punishment for Martin, in fact it was more like a reward. 'He rejoices in going to Belfast prison,' explained the defence counsel. 'It's his very favourite place.'

New York taxpayers are footing the £10,000 bill for killer Jeff 'Giant' Barslow to have his big ears cut down to size to stop him being the butt of unkind jokes. Jail chiefs granted the six foot ten prisoner, also known as Dumbo, plastic surgery to help prevent him from getting into fights.

103

In January 1982, the pride and joy of the US prison system was opened in Baltimore. It was an $11.5 million building, with computer-controlled security systems.

In March, nine inmates escaped by kicking out a glass and plastic window that was supposed to be unbreakable. It quickly became apparent that the wonder jail had one or two other small problems. According to the Chief Guard, Sheriff Charles H Hickey, these were just some of the faults:

- Remote control cameras that were to pan the building had to be turned off after a half-hour and rested for up to two hours for cooling, otherwise the motors burned out.

- Many of the locks either would not lock or, once locked, would not open.

- A mechanical door had malfunctioned and chopped off a guard's fingertip.

- Computer malfunctions had periodically trapped people in various parts of the building.

- Solar panels, installed to provide solar heating, had frozen solid in the winter months and had been totally useless.

- Guards were unable to see into the cells from their guard posts, and the microphones provided to them to talk to the inmates in their cells were largely unusable because of the noise in the cell block.

Sheriff Hickey had made one small adjustment himself – he put a lock on the front door of the prison!

A prisoner in Charleston, South Carolina, escaped by climbing through his cell window and scaling down the wall on a length of dental floss. The man had been buying dental floss from the prison shop and secretly making a rope. Police are looking for a man with appalling teeth.

104

In New York City, a fat, long-haired drunken man was put in the women's police cells for the night, even though cops had strip-searched him first.

The Philippines seem to have cracked the problem of repeat offenders. Just five per cent of the 8,000 inmates at the national prison are repeat offenders – compared to sixty per cent in US jails and fifty per cent in Japanese prisons. The Philippine's director of prisons agreed that one of the reasons was that in Japanese and American jails prisoners receive delicious food, but in the Philippines the prison food is so bad that it acts as a very effective deterrent.

In 1911 a man was condemned to death in the tiny European state of Monaco. The authorities brought in an executioner from France who demanded 10,000 francs for the job. This was far too expensive for Monaco to pay, but the executioner refused to lower his price, and returned to France. They were left with a convicted murderer and a growing bill for his upkeep – he was the only prisoner in the maximum security jail. Finally the governor proposed a deal – if the man promised not to escape, most of the guards would be withdrawn and he would be paid a small allowance to provide for himself. The man agreed and lived in comfort until his death, thirty years later.

From 1791 to 1821, the local jail in the Greek town of Vostitza on the island of Zante, was in the trunk of a tree. The hollow trunk of a giant plane tree had a circumference of over fifty feet and was able to house all of Vostitza's prisoners.

CHAPTER 22

Sporting Fixtures

In Malaya it is against the law to dance on the backs of turtles.

Duelling is illegal in Uruguay – unless both parties are registered blood donors. If this is the case, it is encouraged.

Using water pistols for duelling is illegal in Massachusetts.

Key West, Florida, prohibits turtle races within city limits.

In Hartford, Connecticut, you cannot cross the street while walking on your hands.

A 'Bum-pinching' day held every year since the Middle Ages in Hanshrag, Germany, has been banned after women's libbers complained.

In Nebraska, fishermen must wet their hands before taking fish off the hook, while in New York State anglers can keep their hands dry, but they cannot fish in their gardens.

Fishermen in Illinois must have been an unsporting bunch at one time – it is now illegal for them to use dynamite to catch fish. In Santa Clara, California, you're a criminal if you drug trout in the inland lakes or rivers.

It is illegal to fish for trout from the back of a horse in Washington D.C., but in Idaho it is only giraffe-back fishing that is against the law.

In Denver hunters cannot shoot rabbits from the back window of a streetcar in a city street, and in the rest of Colorado it is illegal to hunt ducks from an aeroplane. Kansas forbids the hunting of ducks with a mule.

It is necessary to have a hunting licence before you can trap a mouse in California.

Wrestlers must not make ugly faces at one another during the course of a public match, at least when they're in California.

In Kentucky, it is illegal to shoot clay pigeons during the breeding season. This must be to prevent clay pigeons from becoming an endangered species. And anyway, when is the breeding season?

After a round of golf in a club in Ohio, Richard Arntzen was furious at his bad performance. He went on a rampage in which he destroyed an electric golf cart, smashed a car with a three iron, clubbed his cousin with a putter, whacked his cousin's friend on the head with a driver, and finally attacked a policeman who came to calm him down. Eventually he had to be tear-gassed and clubbed by police before he could be restrained. He later told police, 'I'm sorry. You know how it is, I had a bad round.'

Juggling is illegal in Hood River, Oregon.

An unsporting law in Tucson, Arizona, states: 'It shall be unlawful for any visiting football team or player to carry, convey, tote, kick, throw, pass or otherwise transport or propel any inflated pigskin across the University of Arizona goal line or score a safety within the confines of the city of Tucson, County of Pima, State of Arizona.'

In Bristol, a women's football team was penalized when they beat a guest men's team. FA officials were forced to discipline the Bristol Rovers Women's Club after the game due to their rough tactics.

In Toltec, Colorado it's a fine for fishermen catching their limit with bare hands; they must use a fishing rod and bait. And don't get caught shooting fish with a gun in Washington State or Hazlehurst, Mississippi or with a bow and arrow in Louisville, Kentucky. Fish must breathe a sigh of relief when they swim into the waters of Knoxville, Tennessee, where it is illegal to lasso a fish.

North Andover, Massachusetts, bars people from carrying 'space guns', so check your weapons when you ask Scotty to beam you down.

In the state of Washington, lawmakers seem to believe in fair play. The law states: 'It is illegal to hunt ducks from a row-boat unless you are upright and visible from the waist up.'

Oklahoma (which is inland) has a law against catching whales in its waters.

It's illegal, in Kentucky, to shoot a gun that isn't loaded.

CHAPTER 23

In Church

Clergyman who fancy themselves comics had better not preach what they practise in Nicholas County, West Virginia, where the police can bar a theologian from cracking jokes, or telling a humorous story from the pulpit during a service.

'Any person who displays, handles or uses any kind of reptile in connection with any religious service or gathering shall be fined not less than fifty dollars nor more than one hundred dollars,' it is stated by the Kentucky legislature.

Two priests took to fisticuffs in the town square of Caltanissetta, Sicily, when one accused the other of stealing his flock. 'He's jealous of my full church,' said Vincenzo Romano, 'When he punched me, I had to defend myself.'

In 1900, fifteen Buddhist idols fell off a temple shelf in China, crushing a man below. The bereaved family took the statues to court, where they were found guilty and sentenced to death by beheading.

In Alabama it is against the law to wear a false moustache in church — if it makes people laugh, that is.

Eight months after his death in 896 AD, the Italian pope, Formosus, was put on trial. His body was exhumed and propped in the defendant's chair while the new pope, Stephen IV, sought to prove that his five-year pontificate had been illegal. Formosus, who did not say much in his own defence, was found guilty and his corpse was stripped of his papal finery and thrown into the Tiber.

James Filewood, a sixteenth-century English cleric and thief, had a lucky escape from execution with the help of a legal exemption which stated: 'If the accused could prove he could read, so he would be branded on the hand and freed.' Filewood was illiterate, but a friend had agreed to whisper the words in his ear. 'Oh Lord', read the friend, pausing for Filewood to repeat his words. Unfortunately, Filewood's thumb was covering the next line of the text, so his friend whispered to him to move it. 'Oh Lord, take away thy thumb,' the dim-witted Filewood repeated out loud. The game was up, but the judge was so amused he spared Filewood's life.

Not one to profit from good fortune, Filewood pursued his career of theft anew. He was arrested and accused of the theft of a watch. Fortunately for Filewood, the stolen article could not be found to be produced as evidence so he was again released from court. Unfortunately for Filewood, an alarm sounded from his pocket calling attention to what proved to be the watch. This time there was no loophole; the watch was returned to its owner, and the not-so-good cleric Filewood was hanged.

Portland, Oregon, forbids men of the cloth to perform wedding ceremonies at skating rinks or inside theatres.

Persistence must run in the Thorat family. They pursued a case asserting the family's right to preside over public functions and precedences at religious festivals, for 761 years, each successive generation taking over the case from the last. On 28 April 1966, Balasaheb Patloji Thorat finally won the case, which had been running since 1205.

CHAPTER 24

Miscellaneous Misdemeanours

In several New England settlements a gentleman could commit the following offences and be fined a sum equivalent of $10 – lie eight times, swear four times, beat his wife twice or criticize a court once.

The carpenter who built the first stocks in Boston in 1634, a gentleman named Palmer, was also the first person to occupy them. He submitted a bill for one pound and thirteen shillings for the work and according to records, 'the town elders felt this to be excessive and hauled Palmer before the court on a charge of profiteering'. He was found guilty, fined a pound and sentenced to spend half an hour in the stocks he built – the elders wanted to try out the new apparatus without delay. Palmer could be considered fortunate – at least he did not invent the guillotine!

Seattle, Washington proclaims it is illegal to carry any concealed weapon over the length of six feet.

A British salesman may be breaking the law and considered a *national nuisance* for attempting to sell a vacuum cleaner to a woman in a public place. The penalty: up to three months in jail! According to the lawmakers it would seem that seeing someone's Hoover in public is more of a nuisance than seeing their etchings in private.

Participants at an anger management course in Madrid failed to put their training into effect. The police were called in after fighting erupted between the delegates and ten people were injured. The fight broke out during a discussion on which methods were most effective in helping to keep tempers cool.

In 1981, during a major case against the Ford Motor Company, the plaintiff's lawyer, in hopes of an even bigger judgement, told his client to forgo Ford's offer of a $2 million settlement made while the jury was out deliberating the case. The jury returned and found Ford not guilty of all charges. The plaintiff is now suing his lawyer.

A Japanese mugger, armed with crossbow, axe, stun gun, smoke grenade and a can of Mace, tripped over his own feet during a getaway from a robbery in Osaka and was arrested.

Detectives in Foggia, Italy, arrested a burglar on the evidence of his earprints. Teenager Massimo Manzi had a habit of listening at the doors of his intended targets and the police used the various ear prints to identify him as the housebreaker. He would have been in even worse trouble in Oklahoma, where eavesdropping is illegal.

In December 1994, a jury deliberated for three hours before ruling against Stewart Blair in the case of Blair vs Poulin. Mr Blair was suing his friend Maurice Poulin for injuries incurred when Blair tripped over a snow-plough blade, claiming that Poulin caused the fall when he startled Blair by accidentally passing gas in his face.

When farmer David Cannon consulted lawyers for advice concerning a civil compensation claim against his local National Westminster Bank, he was told it would take years before the matter could be settled. Furious that he had lost £300,000 as a result of the bank's unauthorised transfer of his funds, he decided that at the age of sixty-seven he could not wait that long for justice. So he returned to the bank and made an unusual deposit – four tonnes of steaming manure. The bank's gleaming stone and glass exterior was covered in the foul smelling mess, and over one foot of manure was dumped in a mound on the pavement. Mr Cannon was arrested for criminal damage, and will not be asking for interest on his deposit.

Helmut Roummels would have sympathised with Farmer Cannon; he had trouble with his bank too. They refused him a loan, so the irate construction worker drove his giant earth-mover from the quarry where he worked to his bank in Hamburg, crashed through the front doors and flattened desks, counter and computers, causing £50,000 worth of damage. He still did not get his loan.

In New York City it is illegal to have a deck of cards in your home if you live within a one mile radius of an armoury.

A bell once received an official pardon – it was sent to Siberia in 1591 for signalling a rebellion and was eventually pardoned and returned home 300 years later.

Michael R Wagoner, of Knoxville Tennessee, shot a man five times in a bar because he thought the man had asked, 'Have you got a light, baby?' The man actually said 'buddy'.

A man has filed suit against the city of San Diego after he saw women using the men's urinals during a concert at the Jack Murphy Stadium. Bob Glaser, a political consultant, is asking for $5.4 million for embarrassment and emotional trauma.

Do you believe in fairies? Before you answer, you should know that in England in the time of Henry III, the penalty for killing, wounding or maiming a fairy was death.

In 1974 Philippe Petit of France was arrested for trespassing. He had been walking along a tightrope stretched between the two towers of the World Trade Center in New York. The rope stretched 1,350 feet (411 metres) above the ground. Before his arrest he had already crossed it seven times.

In Illinois speaking English is illegal. Author H L Mencken established the official language of Illinois as American.

In Leahy, Washington, it is illegal to blow your nose in a public place.

Yugoslavia once passed a law prohibiting Halley's comet from appearing in the sky. The comet managed to comply with this law for seventy-four years!

In Louisiana, it has been deemed perfectly legal to grow just as tall as you wish.

Alabama residents are banned from reading books about outlaws.

The Hawaiians have one of the most sensible laws on the statute books – it is illegal to insert pennies in your ears.

A former cafeteria manager at the Smithsonian Museum in Washington was awarded $400,000 after a jury heard his boss had called him an 'old fart'.

Joseph Stalin tried to ban Christmas trees, but the Soviet population just kept on buying them – so he declared them 'New Year's' trees in order to save face.

Stalin wasn't the first killjoy to try to put a stop to Yuletide cheer. In 1644, Oliver Cromwell's government banned Christmas, calling it 'The Profane Man's Ranting Day'. Massachusetts lawmakers followed suit in 1659, making it a fineable offence to celebrate the season of goodwill.

The Cat Intelligence Test

E. M. Bard

How Clever Is Your Cat?

Can your cat
- Make sounds upon request?
- Predict a change in the weather?

Or is your cat the type who
- Falls off ledges while sleeping?
- Continually runs into walls or doors?

You can find out how smart your cat really is by giving him or her the Cat Intelligence Test – a simple, four-part IQ test. By observation and by using everyday household items you will be able to measure your cat's coordination, communication, social and reasoning powers.

Also includes:
- Suggestions on how to improve your cat's IQ.
- Comparative scores of other cats by age, sex and type.
- A Certificate of Merit to be filled in and proudly displayed on completion of the Cat Intelligence Test.

ISBN 0 00 638328 9

Latin For All Occasions

Henry Beard

Who says Latin is a dead language? The Roman mass may be a thing of the past, but Latin's never been livelier.

Henry Beard, former prisoner of the classics, has produced an essential tool for anyone who's ever struggled with an ablative. Here, in one handy volume, are hundreds of everyday English expressions rendered into grammatically accurate, idiomatically correct, classic Latin and an easy to use pronunciation guide.

Latin For All Occasions gives you the perfect phrase for every contemporary situation from starting a relationship (*Frequentasne hunc locum?* Do you come here often?) to making a swift exit (*Di! Ecce hora! Uxor mea me necabit!* God! Look at the time! My wife will kill me!)

'Humour book of the year' – *The Times*

ISBN 0 00 255383 X

The Official Politically Correct Dictionary and Handbook

Henry Beard and Christopher Cerf

Welcome to the Nineties! But you'd better watch what you say . . .

Do you remember when people were 'dishonest' not 'ethically disorientated', 'drunk' not 'chemically inconvenienced,' 'fat' not 'horizontally challenged' or 'old' not 'experientially enhanced'?

You do? then you must forget such political incorrectnesses – and learn the language of the future. Only with this comprehensive, exhaustively researched reference work can you find out exactly what you can say, what you can't say, who says, and why.

Read this book and never again will you refer to: *the ugly bald shoplifter who is a sadomasochistic wino*. You will be politically correct and say: *the cosmetically different, follicularly challenged nontraditional shopper is a differently pleasured, substance abuse survivor!*

Whether you're oppressor or victim (or both) *The Official Politically Correct Dictionary and Handbook* is essential – and highly entertaining – reading.

ISBN 0 586 21726 6

Henry Beard and Christopher Cerf

Sex and Dating

The Official Politically Correct Guide

If you thought going on a date was simply a question of spending time with the opposite sex – think again! Dating is a consequence of 'phallocratic social conditioning', and before you indulge in such 'heterocentrism', or even 'consensual love-making', you must learn the language and the rules of the be-sensitive-or-else 1990s.

Only Henry Beard and Christopher Cerf can guide you through the politically correct minefield of sexual etiquette – what to do, where to do it, what to call it, who to do it with, and what they'll do to you if you try. Don't even think about calling your significant other until you've read this informative, hilarious and increasingly topical book.

Romance isn't dead, it's just 'terminally inconvenienced'!

0 00 638377 7